Journaling Through the Seasons:

Fall & Faith

Bonnie Liabenow

Journaling through the Seasons
Fall & Faith

Created by Core Communications International
1443 Newport Street #5
Traverse City, Michigan 49686

Published by Word and Spirit Publishing
PO Box 701403, Tulsa, Oklahoma 74170
wordandspiritpublishing.com

ISBN: 978-1-685730-35-2

Cover design: Bobby Chamberlain, www.bobbyccreative.com

Interior design and typeset: Typography Creations

Editor: Mickey Broach

Creative Director & Editor: Meghan Dryzga, www.copymoves.com

Content Advisors: Alyssa Liabenow | Shea Petaja

Printed in the United States of America.

In a world painted with a golden hue,
Where the leaves fall and skies are blue,
Autumn comes with a soft, gentle sigh,
As summer bids its warm goodbye.

The winds whisper secrets to the trees,
As they shed their leaves with graceful ease,
A symphony of colors, a feast for the eyes,
As the world transforms under the skies.

The days grow shorter, the nights grow long,
The world sings a melancholy song,
Yet there is beauty in the change,
As the seasons shift and rearrange.

In the stillness, there is a certain grace,
As the world slows down its frenzied pace,
Autumn comes with a sense of calm,
A soothing balm, a healing salve.

In the midst of change, there is a peace,
A reminder that all things must cease,
But there is beauty in the letting go,
As the world prepares for winter's snow.

— UNKNOWN

Contents

Defining the *Season*

"Like the seasons of nature — winter, spring, summer, and fall — so are the seasons of life. Seasons are specific periods of time, and they vary in length. Some seasons last for a period of years, while others can be just a few short months."
– *Excellence With Simple Elegance*, p. 102

A fall season of life is represented by its brilliance and is themed, "In the Midst of Change".

Change, v.

"to make or become different,"
– Cambridge Dictionary

Change, n.

"the act or instance of making or becoming different." – Oxford Languages

"Blessed be the name of God forever and ever, For wisdom and might are His. And He changes the times and the seasons;" – DANIEL 2: 20 (NKJV)

FAITH, n.

> "complete trust or confidence in someone or something."
>
> "a strong belief in God." – OXFORD LANGUAGES

"Faith is the confident assurance that something we want is going to happen. It is the certainty that what we hope for is waiting for us, even though we cannot see it up ahead." – HEBREWS 11:1 (TLB)

THE *Benefits* OF JOURNALING

WHY JOURNAL?

> *As I look through my past journals, I see how God has been working in my life—and that reminds me that He is constantly present.* – BONNIE LIABENOW

THERE'S something about writing – something about jotting down how we've felt and what we've learned in a fleeting moment on a day that may have seemed otherwise unremarkable. We so often remember the grandest core memories – where God's work was so evident, he seemingly all but showed up and shook hands around the room. But when life moves fast, smaller moments move faster, and even the most joyful ones dissipate to join those now forgotten.

Journaling can preserve them. Journaling can capture and preserve the tireless work of God in our everyday lives so that we may reflect, grow and sometimes just find peace in knowing that He's there. Here are some of the benefits you'll notice as you continue this practice:

- **Objective Reflection**: Journaling is a factual account of your journey. This helps us take a more objective look at our lives and our progress, helping us realize that we are indeed moving ahead.
- **A Safe Space for Emotional Expression**: Journaling provides a private, non-judgmental space for emotional expression and exploration. Your journal is one of the few places you don't have to censor yourself or worry about outside reactions to your thoughts.
- **Stress Management**: Journaling can help manage the stress of juggling multiple roles — employee, parent, spouse, caregiver, etc., we have every day. It can help reduce stress by organizing thoughts and problems, making them feel more manageable.
- **Self-Awareness**: Journaling regularly can help us become more aware of our thoughts, feelings, and behaviors. This can lead to better self-understanding, growth, and personal development.
- **Memory and Cognitive Function**: Journaling can enhance memory and cognitive functions. It encourages the brain to dissect experiences and memories, which can lead to improved comprehension and recall.
- **Healing**: Journaling has been used as a tool in therapeutic settings and for self-help, as writing about traumas or negative experiences can help in the healing process.
- **Empowerment**: Journaling allows each of us to express our personal experiences, ideas, and views freely. It can be a tool for empowerment, helping each of us find our voice in a society where we may feel unheard.

- **Goal Setting and Personal Growth:** Journaling can assist in setting and tracking goals. It can be a great tool for personal growth, helping to monitor progress over time.

HOW WILL THIS HELP ME GROW IN MY FAITH?

> *When you reflect on how good God is—and all the great things He has done, is doing, and even will do in your life—there's a natural sense of gratefulness. Documenting these moments protects you from ever taking for granted the love and mercy of God in your life—the moments that so quickly fade are great blessings, and they are enough to keep us amazed.* – BONNIE LIABENOW

The habit of journaling can strengthen your spiritual walk as it encourages you to dedicate time to your faith, beliefs, and spiritual insights. Your journal allows you to identify what is starving your spirit and brings quietness to a busy day.

WHERE DO I START?

> *I write down verses that encourage me, some of the prayer requests I'm praying that day, things I feel like the Lord is putting on my heart, and the good things that God does for me. If I want to hear God speak to me, the first thing I do is say, "God, I want you to speak to me. Hearing from you is not just nice, it is a necessity!" And then I withdraw and get alone and quiet. ("Be still and know that I am God.") And then I wait quietly, patiently, and expectantly on God. I ask a specific question, I look into his Word and then when I see God's answer, I write it down. Habakkuk said, "The Lord gave me this answer, 'Write down clearly... what I reveal to you...'"* – BONNIE LIABENOW

Choose one of the topics below that resonates most with you. Start small so you don't feel overwhelmed, and take it just one sentence at a time. Length of entry doesn't matter–only your authenticity. You can:

- Write about the goodness of God in your life!
- Write about a tough situation when God has protected and guided you
- Keep a record of your petitions and blessings
- Make it a gratitude journal of your words of praise and worship using the different names for God provided in the prompts given

Not every day will look the same, and that's welcomed and expected.

Tips for Journaling

- **Redefine journaling.** This is not the same as keeping a diary. A diary is, 'Dear diary, this is what I did today.' A journal is, 'This is what I learned today.'
- **Write spiritual encounters.** If it's on your heart, don't hesitate to write it down. All spiritual encounters with the most Holy God are worthy of documenting.
- **Write your heartfelt response.** Start by reading scripture [each psalm] two or three times with the prayerful question in mind: *What does God want me to hear, read, or see from this? How does this resonate with me? As I meditate on the words, what stands out? Does it provide answers? Does it raise questions?* Or *does it not resonate at all, and why?* Ask God for clarity in these lines.
- **Same time.** Set a time each day to sit and self-reflect on your journey. You may look at how you are feeling and

examine why you feel that way. You can also write down things that inspire you throughout the day.

- **Read for inspiration.** Reading your daily writing can help you work toward new goals, search for more answers to questions you've had in the last month, and give thanks for the lessons you've already learned.
- **Set goals.** Setting goals can inspire you. These can be things you wish to do on a daily basis to further your personal growth or things you hope to do within a certain amount of time. Refer to *Excellence with Simple Elegance, Chapter: Goal Setting, Page 145* and also *The Study* for more guidance.
- **Practice gratitude.** It helps to create a thankful heart. Acknowledge your blessings. Write about the things in your day that make you feel grateful. Research shows that people who make a point to feel gratitude are happier and healthier people.
- **Document.** Write down accounts in which you see God working in your life like answers to prayers, and God's favor and blessings given to you. Journaling brings awareness of God's presence in our life, especially that God shows up in both Big ways and small blessings.
- **Take it with you.** Keep your journal with you at all times. Keeping your journal on hand allows you to write down quotes, spiritual text references, or general thoughts you wish to reflect on right when they come to mind.
- **Look back.** Review your journal entries at least once a month. By taking time to self-reflect on your prior entries, you can better see the direction you're heading in spiritual enlightenment.

- **Be authentic.** The Book of Psalms is a great example of journal writing. David took the first five books of the Bible: Genesis, Exodus, Leviticus, Numbers, Deuteronomy, and he meditated on them day and night and wrote his prayers down. As you read the Psalms, you'll see that David includes just about every emotion known to the human race including envy, jealousy, lust, and greed. David is brutally honest in his writing; he does not write what he thinks, he writes what he honestly feels. This paves a path of authenticity, setting a powerful example for us in our own journaling.
- **Enjoy It.**

A Note on *Fall* and Its *Brilliance*

by Meghan Dryzga

I see it now. I hadn't. Not before. I mean, given the way Bonnie entered my life the first time around, I absolutely should've known. *He has a way of getting through to us, doesn't He?*

It was a blazing hot day in June, and I was sitting atop a rickety set of metal bleachers beside a field of 50-some children where my four-year-old was loosely attempting to represent the game of soccer. I was spread mother-of-four thin and steeped in frustration from an uninspiring workday, spewing words of loathing and disdain to fellow soccer moms between barks of faux-fully cheerful encouragement and water breaks.

Bonnie's phone number lit up my screen and rattled my phone along the bench. "Hi, Bonnie!" I answered cheerfully, as the claws of anxiety nearly reached in and stole my breath. *When will you find the time, Meghan?!, the voice of anxiety whispered.* But, I knew this fast-talking, falsely well-intentioned voice; It's the voice that climbs inside my mind and jockeys me back toward life's routines, seemingly numbing my mind's penchant for therapeutic writing, clarity and a-ha moments. I stood up off the bench, perhaps symbolically, to quiet down the voice inside my head, if only for long enough to hear Bonnie's voice rise above the din of the field to say, "fall." *She invited me to write about fall!*

Oh, how I wanted to write about fall. I stared at the bank of trees just a few yards beyond the fields, thick and unmoving in the stagnant summer air. And while fall may have seemed light-years away for most, I could just envision the very trees I looked upon, ignited in brilliant fall colors.

Goosebumps arose on my skin.

"Well, I think there's something really amazing about fall, Bonnie," I said. "Just when it seems life's run out, that's when the forest becomes its most brilliant." Like so many of the thoughts and words and poems and lyrics that just sort of float down and into my head from a kingdom beyond, I didn't know where this one came from either. Not at the time.

I should've known. I should've known something was coming.

And sure enough, it took me months between soccer practices and back-to-school preparations and anxious whispers to allow myself the moments to be still, and listen. *Be still and listen. Write down what you heard.*

What happens next is... well, it's both heart-wrenching and remarkable; it's both obvious and unbelievable. It's the reason, the purpose... the unparalleled, world-rocking impact of journaling.

"Sorry, guys, I have to take this call. My stepmom is waiting on some test results," I told my boss and colleagues as I quickly traded one call for the other. My dad and stepmom's voices were steady on the phone at first; then pauses between words stretched to uncomfortable lengths before their voices were drenched in despair. Atop a crushing diagnosis, the doctors had stacked a finite timeline. No one — not anyone — was prepared.

I imagined I'd boarded the Himalaya at the county fair. Thoughts came at me as fast as the wind and as wild as the lyrics of the songs blaring over carnival speakers. I wasn't sure which lyrics to chase, and by the 23rd time around, I just wanted off the ride. *I don't want this. I don't want any of this.*

I couldn't solve it. There wasn't a solution. That's just not how I operate; "Don't bring problems without solutions," I'd tell my team at work. And here I was, states away from my parents, helpless. I took the evening to regroup; after coming completely undone, I attempted to assemble a plan.

Just when it seems life's run out, that's when the forest becomes its most brilliant.

That night, I texted my stepmom. "I commit to brightening every day — if only for a moment — with laughter, happiness, love and/or the foolishness of your grandchildren," I wrote in a text message, smiling through tears. So I went on to collect stories, videos, photos, and a list of Amazon deliveries that might bring her joy. I've since delivered one every day. See, I'm no good at sadness, but I drafted the blueprints to a house built on loud laughter, sarcasm, clever quips and smiles.

I see it now — God's work in my life. I hadn't before I wrote it down. How quickly events like these can turn our thoughts to hate, to doubt, to abandonment. Had I not put down the words, the feelings, the visions and wild autumn metaphors that fluttered into my brain that summer day months ago, it would all be lost… a colossal misunderstanding. *I see it now.* He was preparing me for how to cope with the inevitable. For how to deliver brilliance and joy, how to embrace my mom in the briskness of the autumn breeze and guide her eyes up to the colors at their most brilliant. How to inspire everyone around her to shine radiantly through the seasons that test our resilience most.

I can confidently say, I've never been so acutely aware of God's presence and felt so much gratitude for it. In the journal prompts that follow, Bonnie reminds us, there's so much of His work that's worthy of our reflection. Occasions that would otherwise be missed or forgotten.

Oh — I never mentioned how Bonnie first entered my life 10 years ago, did I? See, she was steeped in God-given purpose to publish some powerful faith-based writing in Excellence with Simple Elegance, and wanted me to write the foreword; meanwhile, I had no idea she and her faith-strengthening tools were intentionally God-placed in my path.

Second verse, same as the first (ehem, see paragraph two).

So how could a spread-thin mother of four like me possibly remember a series of parallel events from 10 years ago, and know so well our Lord and Savior had — clearly — settled in for another meal at our table? I'll give you a hint: I sat back down with the foreword I wrote 10 years ago like it was my journal from decades past, and simply read what I wrote down.

May you also experience the power of journaling in faith.

A Fall Song of *Worship* and *Praise*

Inspired by Psalm 122, 123 & 124

Jehovah-'Immeku "Lord Is With You" — Judges 6:12

Yeah for Sunday! I was so glad when they said to me, "Let us go into the house of the Lord." Praise be to the Lord.

If the Lord had not been on my side when people came against me, they would have swallowed me alive. The flood of critics would have engulfed me, tormented me and swept me away in the raging waters of their anger. I have escaped like a bird, but not by my strength. My help is in the name of the Lord, the Maker of heaven and earth

Unto You, O Lord, I lift up my eyes to the heavens. As the eyes of a servant look to the hand of her master and the eyes of a maid to the hand of her mistress, so my eyes stay on You, my God, where I find strength, mercy and comfort. Continue to have mercy on me, O Lord. I still struggle. I am exceedingly filled with contempt and anger to those who find joy in tormenting me. I am desperate for Your strength, Your mercy and Your comfort.

I pray for peace to calm me. Let me prosper for I love you. Let peace rain within the walls of my home and prosperity come to the work of my hand. I will lift up my eyes to the hills—From whence comes my help? My help comes from the Lord, Who made heaven and earth. You, O Lord, are my keeper; You are my shade. The sun will not strike me by day, nor the moon by night. You will preserve me from all evil; You will preserve my soul. You will preserve my going out and my coming in from this time forth, and even forevermore.

Yeah for Sunday! I was glad when they said to me, "Let us go into the house of the Lord."

Response:

A Fall Song of *Worship* and *Praise*

Highlight and Respond below

Inspired by Psalm 122, 123 & 124

Jehovah-'Immeku "Lord Is With You" – Judges 6:12

YEAH for Sunday! I was so glad when they said to me, "Let us go into the house of the Lord." Praise be to the Lord.

If the Lord had not been on my side when people came against me, they would have swallowed me alive. The flood of critics would have engulfed me, tormented me and swept me away in the raging waters of their anger. I have escaped like a bird, but not by my strength. My help is in the name of the Lord, the Maker of heaven and earth

Unto You, O Lord, I lift up my eyes to the heavens. As the eyes of a servant look to the hand of her master and the eyes of a maid to the hand of her mistress, so my eyes stay on You, my God, where I find strength, mercy and comfort. Continue to have mercy on me, O Lord. I still struggle. I am exceedingly filled with contempt and anger to those who find joy in tormenting me. I am desperate for Your strength, Your mercy and Your comfort.

I pray for peace to calm me. Let me prosper for I love you. Let peace rain within the walls of my home and prosperity come to the work of my hand. I will lift up my eyes to the hills—From whence comes my help? My help comes from the Lord, Who made heaven and earth. You, O Lord, are my keeper; You are my shade. The sun will not strike me by day, nor the moon by night. You will preserve me from all evil; You will preserve my soul. You will preserve my going out and my coming in from this time forth, and even forevermore.

Yeah for Sunday! I was glad when they said to me, "Let us go into the house of the Lord."

Reflection:

"The trees are about to show us how lovely it is to let things go."
—Jane Lee Logan

Healing:

God commands trees to let go of all their leaves. What are you to let go of? Write within the leaves.

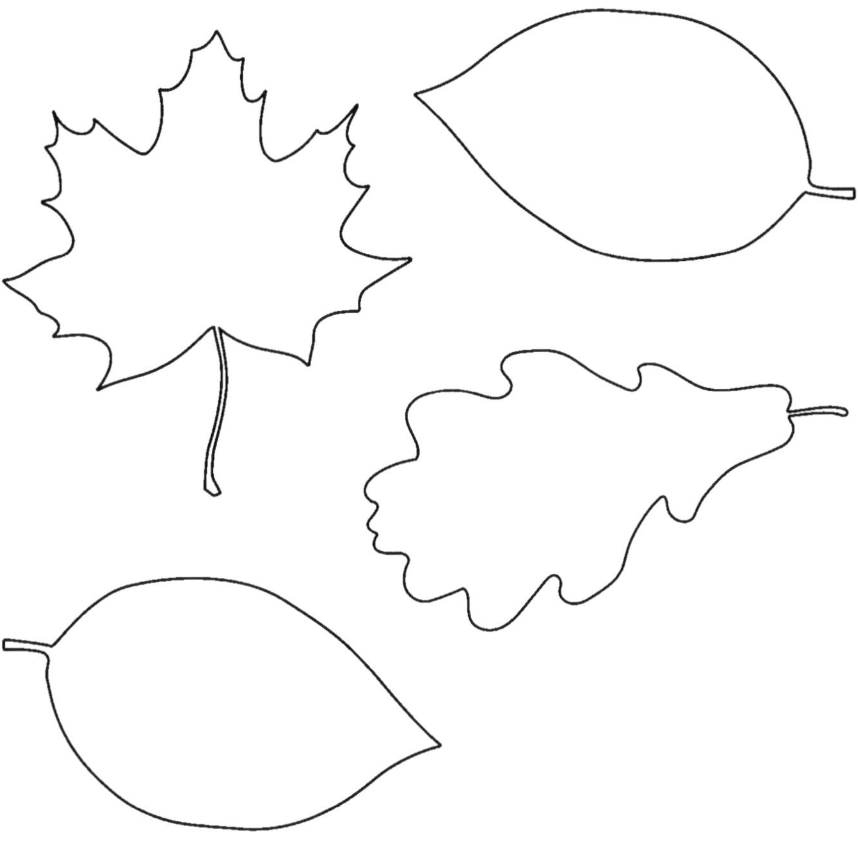

Notes

Notes

Notes

A Fall Prayer of *Petition* and *Blessing*

Inspired by Psalm 27 & 86

Jehovah-Chatsahi — Lord my Strength of my life

Hear, O Lord, and answer me. I am hurting. Once again, this storm is raging against me. I need Your gentle touch. You are my God. My faith and hope is in You. O Lord, please embrace me with Your extravagant unending love as I cry out for You. Bring calm to my chaos and return my joy. Strengthen my heart and show me Your favor. Hear my prayer, O Lord, and listen to my cry.

Whom shall I fear? The Lord is the strength of my life;

Though trouble is against me, My heart shall not fear;

Though chaos rises against me, In You I will be confident.

There is One thing I desire; let me dwell in Your house, O Lord, and may I see Your beauty. Teach me Your ways so I will be faithful to walk in Your truth. Let my life bring honor to Your name.

In my time of trouble, take me to the secret place and hide me. Show Your mercy to me and answer me. It is Your face I seek. I will wait on You and in the waiting I will lift up my soul and worship You. O Lord my God, there is no one like You.

Happiness and blessing comes to one who gives up sin. The woman who embraces the instruction of Your Word experiences the provision of a circle of quiet within the clamor of evil.

You give me rest from days of trouble. Your loving kindness holds me up, O Lord. When my worry is great within me, Your comfort brings joy to my soul.

You will never walk away from Your people. Rest assured that justice is on its way. Yes, O Lord, You are our strong place and the rock where we are safe. O Lord our God, there is no one like You.

Response:

A Fall Prayer of *Petition* and *Blessing*

Highlight and Respond below

Inspired by Psalm 27 & 86

Jehovah-Chatsahi – Lord my Strength of my life

Hear, O Lord, and answer me. I am hurting. Once again, this storm is raging against me. I need Your gentle touch. You are my God. My faith and hope is in You. O Lord, please embrace me with Your extravagant unending love as I cry out for You. Bring calm to my chaos and return my joy. Strengthen my heart and show me Your favor. Hear my prayer, O Lord, and listen to my cry.

Whom shall I fear? The Lord is the strength of my life;
Though trouble is against me, My heart shall not fear;
Though chaos rises against me, In You I will be confident.

There is One thing I desire; let me dwell in Your house, O Lord, and may I see Your beauty. Teach me Your ways so I will be faithful to walk in Your truth. Let my life bring honor to Your name.

In my time of trouble, take me to the secret place and hide me. Show Your mercy to me and answer me. It is Your face I seek. I will wait on You and in the waiting I will lift up my soul and worship You. O Lord my God, there is no one like You.

Happiness and blessing comes to one who gives up sin. The woman who embraces the instruction of Your Word experiences the provision of a circle of quiet within the clamor of evil.

You give me rest from days of trouble. Your loving kindness holds me up, O Lord. When my worry is great within me, Your comfort brings joy to my soul.

You will never walk away from Your people. Rest assured that justice is on its way. Yes, O Lord, You are our strong place and the rock where we are safe. O Lord our God, there is no one like You.

Reflection:

> *"We all face storms in life. Some are more difficult than others, but we all go through trials and tribulation. That's why we have the gift of faith."* —JOYCE MEYER

Self-awareness:

As you face the storms of life and the whirlwind changes, what is your greatest need? Identify the trial you are facing and the need that accompanies it within each aspect of your life listed.

Spiritual: ______________________________

____

____

____

____

____

____

Emotional: ______________________________

____

____

____

____

____

____

Mental:

Physical

What resources are available to you to meet these needs?

Notes

Notes

Notes

A Fall Song of *Worship* and *Praise*

Inspired by Psalm 135 & 136

Jehovah-Elyon — Lord Most High, Your loving-kindness never ends.

Thank you Lord, for You are so good! Your faithful love lasts forever.

Thank you Lord, for You are the God of gods. Your faithful love lasts forever.

Thank you Lord, for You are the Lord of lords. Your faithful love lasts forever.

Praise Your holy name!

I will stand within the walls of Your house. I will Praise Your name for You are good. I will sing praises to Your name, for it is sweet.

Thank you Lord, for You alone do mighty miracles. Your faithful love lasts forever.

Thank you Lord, for You made the heavens so skillfully. Your faithful love lasts forever.

Thank you Lord, for You placed the earth among the waters. Your faithful love lasts forever. I know that You are great. You are greater than all gods. You do whatever is pleasing to You, in heaven and on earth, in the seas and in all waters.

Thank you Lord, You who made the heavenly lights—Your faithful love lasts forever. The sun to rule the day, and the moon and stars to rule the night. Your faithful love lasts forever.

You make the clouds rise from the ends of the earth. You make lightning come with the rain. You bring the wind out from where You store Your riches.

O Lord, Your name lasts forever and will be remembered for all time. I give honor, praise and thanks to You for Your faithful love lasts forever.

Response:

A Fall Song of *Worship* and *Praise*

Highlight and Respond below

Inspired by Psalm 135 & 136

Jehovah-Elyon – Lord Most High, Your loving-kindness never ends.

Thank you Lord, for You are so good! Your faithful love lasts forever.

Thank you Lord, for You are the God of gods. Your faithful love lasts forever.

Thank you Lord, for You are the Lord of lords. Your faithful love lasts forever.

Praise Your holy name!

I will stand within the walls of Your house. I will Praise Your name for You are good. I will sing praises to Your name, for it is sweet.

Thank you Lord, for You alone do mighty miracles. Your faithful love lasts forever.

Thank you Lord, for You made the heavens so skillfully. Your faithful love lasts forever.

Thank you Lord, for You placed the earth among the waters. Your faithful love lasts forever. I know that You are great. You are greater than all gods. You do whatever is pleasing to You, in heaven and on earth, in the seas and in all waters.

Thank you Lord, You who made the heavenly lights—Your faithful love lasts forever. The sun to rule the day, and the moon and stars to rule the night. Your faithful love lasts forever.

You make the clouds rise from the ends of the earth. You make lightning come with the rain. You bring the wind out from where You store Your riches.

O Lord, Your name lasts forever and will be remembered for all time. I give honor, praise and thanks to You for Your faithful love lasts forever.

Reflection:

> *"Love is a fruit in season at all times and within reach of every hand."* – Mother Teresa

Stress management:

Reflect on the roles below and circle the ones that bring about stress…

- Spouse
- Parent
- Employee
- Friend
- Caregiver
- Sister / Brother
- Daughter / Son
- Grandparent

How has your relationship with God made you move to be a more loving person in the roles you've circled? Write within the leaves.

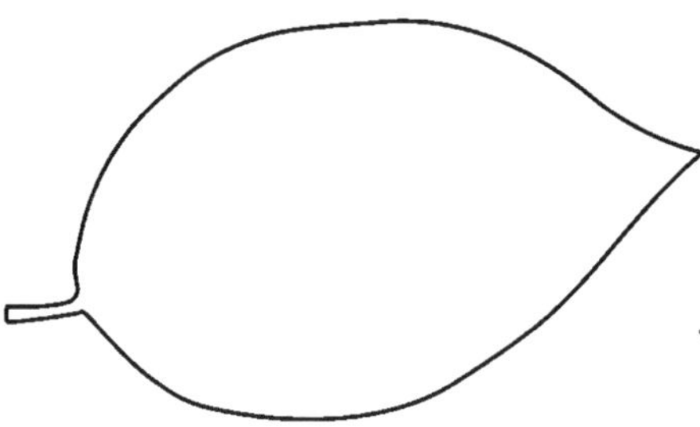

Notes

Notes

Notes

A Fall Prayer of *Petition* and *Blessing*

Inspired by Psalm 11, 12 & 13

Jehovah-Ganan – The Lord Our Defense—a Safe Place

Come quickly, Lord! For God-like people are here no more. The faithful can no longer be seen. So many lies are spoken. Their lips speak with sweet-sounding words that are not true.

I will run for dear life straight into Your arms. You are my only defense. You haven't moved and are always the same. Your holy address hasn't changed. As always, Your eyes take everything in, unblinking, examining inside and out, not missing a thing. You test the good and the bad alike; if anyone cheats, You are outraged. Fail Your test and a person is out, out in a hail of firestones, drinking from a canteen filled with hot desert wind.

Your business is putting things right; You love setting us straight. Once we're standing tall, we can look You straight in the eye. O Lord, You will keep us. You will keep us safe forever from the people of this day.

I choose to put my trust in Your loving kindness. My heart will be full of joy because You will save me. I will sing to You because You have been good to me. In You, I am safe.

Oh, Lord, Your throne is in heaven. Your eyes see as You test everyone. You test and prove those who are right and good and those who are sinful and Your soul hates the one who loves to hurt others.

For You, Oh Lord, love what is right and good. Those who are right with You will see Your face and hear Your Words that are pure, like silver. O Lord, our Defender, keep us in Your loving care. Keep us safe forever from the people of this day. Amen

Response:

A Fall Prayer of *Petition* and *Blessing*

Highlight and Respond below

Inspired by Psalm 11, 12 & 13

Jehovah-Ganan – The Lord Our Defense—a Safe Place

Come quickly, Lord! For God-like people are here no more. The faithful can no longer be seen. So many lies are spoken. Their lips speak with sweet-sounding words that are not true.

I will run for dear life straight into Your arms. You are my only defense. You haven't moved and are always the same. Your holy address hasn't changed. As always, Your eyes take everything in, unblinking, examining inside and out, not missing a thing. You test the good and the bad alike; if anyone cheats, You are outraged. Fail Your test and a person is out, out in a hail of firestones, drinking from a canteen filled with hot desert wind.

Your business is putting things right; You love setting us straight. Once we're standing tall, we can look You straight in the eye. O Lord, You will keep us. You will keep us safe forever from the people of this day.

I choose to put my trust in Your loving kindness. My heart will be full of joy because You will save me. I will sing to You because You have been good to me. In You, I am safe.

Oh, Lord, Your throne is in heaven. Your eyes see as You test everyone. You test and prove those who are right and good and those who are sinful and Your soul hates the one who loves to hurt others.

For You, Oh Lord, love what is right and good. Those who are right with You will see Your face and hear Your Words that are pure, like silver. O Lord, our Defender, keep us in Your loving care. Keep us safe forever from the people of this day. Amen

Reflection:

"Autumn paints emotion like no other season."
– Angie Weiland Crosby

Memory & Cognition:

Describe a place or time you've felt unsafe.

Think of a place that brings forth feelings of warmth and safety.

How might you call upon feelings of God's safety to feel safe even when you feel uneasy?

Notes

Notes

Notes

Notes

A Fall Song of *Worship* and *Praise*

Inspired by Psalm 89

Jehovah-Yasha "The Lord is our Savior"

Your love, God, is my song, and I will sing it!

I will forever speak of Your faithfulness. I will forever tell the story of Your love. I will rejoice all day long in Your wonderful reputation and in Your perfect righteousness. Your love will be built up in me forever and ever.

O God, let the heavens praise Your wonderful ways.

Let the choir of angels sing anthems to Your faithfulness! You are honored in the heavens, Lord God of all, powerful Lord. The evidence of Your faithfulness is all around. You rule the rising sea; its waves rise and You quiet them. The heavens are Yours. The earth is Yours. You made everything that I can see and more. You have made it all from nothing. Your hand is powerful.

Your throne, O Lord, is founded on two strong pillars: justice and righteousness. These pillars are my strength. Mercy and truth walk before You. Your divine favor is my treasure. You are my Father, my God and the Rock that continues to save me.

Response:

A Fall Song of *Worship* and *Praise*

Highlight and Respond below

Inspired by Psalm 89

Jehovah-Yasha "The Lord is our Savior"

Your love, God, is my song, and I will sing it!

I will forever speak of Your faithfulness. I will forever tell the story of Your love. I will rejoice all day long in Your wonderful reputation and in Your perfect righteousness. Your love will be built up in me forever and ever.

O God, let the heavens praise Your wonderful ways.

Let the choir of angels sing anthems to Your faithfulness! You are honored in the heavens, Lord God of all, powerful Lord. The evidence of Your faithfulness is all around. You rule the rising sea; its waves rise and You quiet them. The heavens are Yours. The earth is Yours. You made everything that I can see and more. You have made it all from nothing. Your hand is powerful.

Your throne, O Lord, is founded on two strong pillars: justice and righteousness. These pillars are my strength. Mercy and truth walk before You. Your divine favor is my treasure. You are my Father, my God and the Rock that continues to save me.

Reflection:

She is drawn to grace, the everlasting leaves of change."
– Angie Weiland Crosby

Empowerment:

In 2 Timothy 1: 7 "God has not given us a spirit of fear, but of power, and of love, and of a sound mind."

As a person of faith you have access to God's grace and favor, for every situation.

So Stay strong, stand up and speak out! for what's right and good.

Write to these 4 topics and choose 1 topic that you are passionate about.

Within the leaves freely express your personal experience, ideas and views on these 5 topics

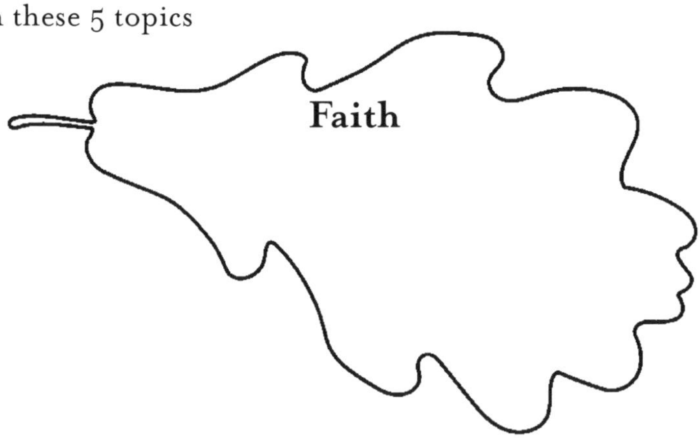

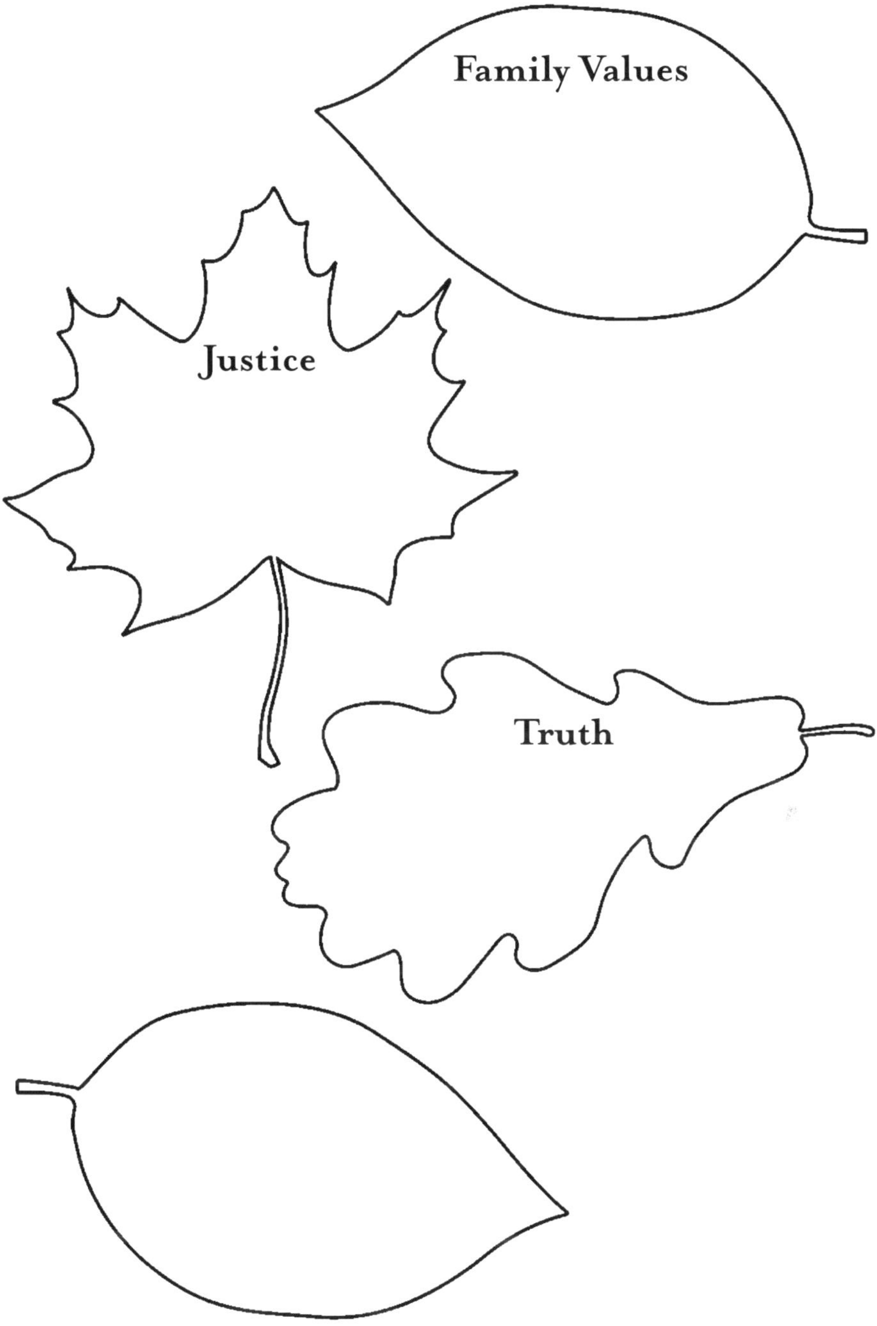
Family Values
Justice
Truth

Notes

Notes

Notes

A Fall Prayer of *Petition* and *Blessing*

Inspired by Psalm 116, 127 & 128

Jehovah-Shalom –Prince of Peace – Isaiah 9:6

I love the Lord, because He has heard my voice and my supplications. He has inclined His ear to me, therefore I will call upon Him as long as I live.

Unless the Lord builds the house, your work is for nothing. Unless the Lord watches over the city, those who watch over it stay awake for nothing.

You rise up early, go to bed late and work hard for your food, all for nothing.

For the Lord gives to His loved ones even while they sleep. May you have His peace!

Prosperity and joy are given to those who fear the Lord—all who follow His ways!

You will enjoy the fruit of your labor. How joyful and prosperous you will be!

You will be like a fruitful grapevine, flourishing within your home.

Your children will be like vigorous young olive trees as they sit around your table.

That is the Lord's blessing for those who fear Him.

May you have His peace!

Our children are a gift from the Lord. They are truly a special reward. The happiness they bring to our homes is one of many blessings.

May the Lord continually bless you. May you prosper as long as you live. May you live to enjoy your grandchildren.

May you have His peace!

Response:

A Fall Prayer of *Petition* and *Blessing*

Highlight and Respond below

Inspired by Psalm 116, 127 & 128

Jehovah-Shalom –Prince of Peace – Isaiah 9:6

I love the Lord, because He has heard my voice and my supplications. He has inclined His ear to me, therefore I will call upon Him as long as I live.

Unless the Lord builds the house, your work is for nothing. Unless the Lord watches over the city, those who watch over it stay awake for nothing.

You rise up early, go to bed late and work hard for your food, all for nothing.

For the Lord gives to His loved ones even while they sleep. May you have His peace!

Prosperity and joy are given to those who fear the Lord—all who follow His ways!

You will enjoy the fruit of your labor. How joyful and prosperous you will be!

You will be like a fruitful grapevine, flourishing within your home.

Your children will be like vigorous young olive trees as they sit around your table.

That is the Lord's blessing for those who fear Him.

May you have His peace!

Our children are a gift from the Lord. They are truly a special reward. The happiness they bring to our homes is one of many blessings.

May the Lord continually bless you. May you prosper as long as you live. May you live to enjoy your grandchildren.

May you have His peace!

Reflection:

Autumn whispers leaf by leaf. Give love to others. Fall in peace."
– ANGIE WEILAND CROSBY

Emotional expression:

Reflect on difficult situations within which you've come to find peace. Which ones can you release and let fall away?

A situation within your family.

A situation within your community.

A situation at work

A situation with your health

Describe the peace that comes with you releasing and letting go.

Notes

Notes

Notes

A Fall Song of *Worship* and *Praise*

Inspired by Psalm 96

The Lord and our Savior calls us to worship Him

I will sing to you, Lord, a song from my heart. I will encourage all that I know to sing to You. Every day I will sing to You. I will honor Your name with my praise and worship. I know I have been called to make Your saving power known as part of my daily routine.

God, You are great and deserve to be given much praise. I will only honor You, Lord.

I will not honor any false gods. I will tell of Your shining greatness in my world. I will tell everyone I know of Your wonderful goodness and blessings on my life. Lord, I am aware of Your wonderful creation. I see Your power in the night sky. You made the heavens.

God, You are great and deserve to be given much praise. I will only honor You, Lord.

Honor and great power are Yours, O Lord. Strength and beauty are in Your holy place. I will offer myself as a gift to You, Lord. I surrender my life for Your purpose. As I worship You, Lord, I realize I am unrighteous and unholy. I desire to mirror and to reflect Your holiness. Cleanse me from all ungodliness.

God, You are great and deserve to be given much praise. I will only honor You, Lord.

Response:

A Fall Song of *Worship* and *Praise*

Highlight and Respond below

Inspired by Psalm 96

The Lord and our Savior calls us to worship Him

I will sing to you, Lord, a song from my heart. I will encourage all that I know to sing to You. Every day I will sing to You. I will honor Your name with my praise and worship. I know I have been called to make Your saving power known as part of my daily routine.

God, You are great and deserve to be given much praise. I will only honor You, Lord.

I will not honor any false gods. I will tell of Your shining greatness in my world. I will tell everyone I know of Your wonderful goodness and blessings on my life. Lord, I am aware of Your wonderful creation. I see Your power in the night sky. You made the heavens.

God, You are great and deserve to be given much praise. I will only honor You, Lord.

Honor and great power are Yours, O Lord. Strength and beauty are in Your holy place. I will offer myself as a gift to You, Lord. I surrender my life for Your purpose. As I worship You, Lord, I realize I am unrighteous and unholy. I desire to mirror and to reflect Your holiness. Cleanse me from all ungodliness.

God, You are great and deserve to be given much praise. I will only honor You, Lord.

Reflection:

> *"We must show our Christian colors if we are to be true to Jesus Christ".* – C.S. Lewis

Personal growth:

We have been called to be His image bearer.

Choose 5 fruits of the spirit (Galatians 5:22,23)

Identify any areas that you need to improve on to reflect His image,

- Love
- Peace
- Goodness
- Gentleness
- Joy
- Patience
- Faithfulness
- Self-control

Write each of the five in a leaf below. Then briefly share how you will shine brilliantly with your spiritual colors this season. (Color each leaf with a colored pencil with your favorite fall color.)

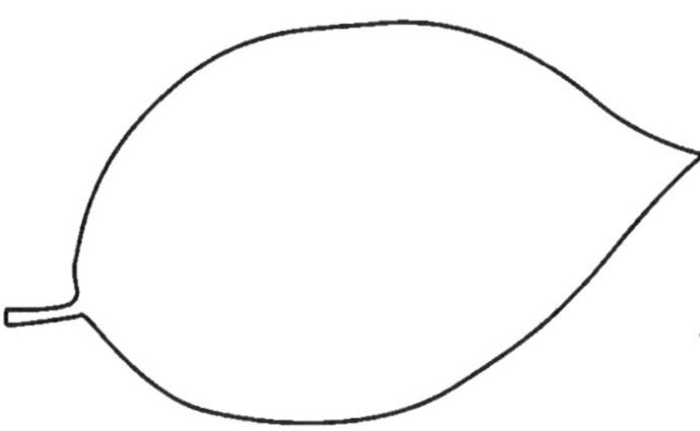

Notes

Notes

Notes

A Prayer of *Petition* and *Blessing*

Inspired by Psalm 39, 54 & 71

Jehovah-Jireh – Provider

And my God will give you everything you need because of His great riches in Christ Jesus. Philippians 4:19 (NLV)

A Prayer of a mature Woman: "Do not be far from me"

And now, Lord, what do I wait for? Save me from all my sins. O Lord, hear my prayer and listen to my cry. Do not be quiet when You see my tears so I may have joy again before I go and am no more.

I have a safe place in you, O Lord. Let me never be ashamed. I will be glad to give You a gift on the altar. I will give thanks to Your name, O Lord, for it is good. For You have taken me out of all trouble. And my eyes have looked without fear.

Because You are right and good, take me out of any trouble I may have brought upon myself. Turn Your ear to me and save me. Be a rock to me where I live, where I may always come and where I will be safe.

For You are my hope, O Lord God. You are my trust since I was young. You have kept me safe from birth. It was You Who watched over me from the day I was born. My praise is always of You.

And now, Lord, what do I wait for? Save me from all my sins. O Lord, hear my prayer and listen to my cry. Do not be quiet when You see my tears so I may have joy again before I go and am no more.

Do not be far from me! Save me by Your name, O God. And stand with me by Your power. Hear my prayer, O God. Listen to the words of my mouth. You are my Helper. You are the One Who keeps my soul alive. I will always have hope and I will praise You more and more. My mouth will tell about how right and good You are and about Your saving acts all day long for there are more than I can know. I will come in the strength of You, Lord. I will tell about how right and good You are and You alone.

And now, Lord, what do I wait for? My hope is in You. Save me from all my sins. O Lord, hear my prayer and listen to my cry. Do not be quiet when You see my tears so I may have joy again before I go and am no more.

You have taught me from when I was young. And I will faithfully tell about Your great works. Even as I grow old and my hair is turning white, O God, please do not leave me alone. Let me be a testament of Your strength to those I love and a testament about Your power to all who are to come. O God, You are right and good, as the heavens are high. You have done great things, O God. Who is like You?

O Lord, let me know my end and how many days I have to live. Let me know that I do not have long to stay here. You have made each of my days as long as a hand is wide. My whole life is nothing in Your eyes. Everyone is only a breath, at best. They walk here and there like a shadow. They store up riches, not knowing who will gather them.

And now, Lord, what do I wait for? My hope is in You. Save me from all my sins. O Lord, hear my prayer and listen to my cry. Do not be quiet when You see my tears so I may have joy again before I go and am no more.

Response:

A Prayer of *Petition* and *Blessing*

Highlight and Respond below

Inspired by Psalm 39, 54 & 71

Jehovah-Jireh — Provider

And my God will give you everything you need because of His great riches in Christ Jesus. Philippians 4:19 (NLV)

A Prayer of a mature Woman: "Do not be far from me"

And now, Lord, what do I wait for? Save me from all my sins. O Lord, hear my prayer and listen to my cry. Do not be quiet when You see my tears so I may have joy again before I go and am no more.

I have a safe place in you, O Lord. Let me never be ashamed. I will be glad to give You a gift on the altar. I will give thanks to Your name, O Lord, for it is good. For You have taken me out of all trouble. And my eyes have looked without fear.

Because You are right and good, take me out of any trouble I may have brought upon myself. Turn Your ear to me and save me. Be a rock to me where I live, where I may always come and where I will be safe.

For You are my hope, O Lord God. You are my trust since I was young. You have kept me safe from birth. It was You Who watched over me from the day I was born. My praise is always of You.

And now, Lord, what do I wait for? Save me from all my sins. O Lord, hear my prayer and listen to my cry. Do not be quiet when You see my tears so I may have joy again before I go and am no more.

Do not be far from me! Save me by Your name, O God. And stand with me by Your power. Hear my prayer, O God. Listen to the words of my mouth. You are my Helper. You are the One Who keeps my soul alive. I will always have hope and I will praise You more and more. My mouth will tell about how right and good You are and about Your saving acts all day long for there are more than I can know. I will come in the strength of You, Lord. I will tell about how right and good You are and You alone.

And now, Lord, what do I wait for? My hope is in You. Save me from all my sins. O Lord, hear my prayer and listen to my cry. Do not be quiet when You see my tears so I may have joy again before I go and am no more.

You have taught me from when I was young. And I will faithfully tell about Your great works. Even as I grow old and my hair is turning white, O God, please do not leave me alone. Let me be a testament of Your strength to those I love and a testament about Your power to all who are to come. O God, You are right and good, as the heavens are high. You have done great things, O God. Who is like You?

O Lord, let me know my end and how many days I have to live. Let me know that I do not have long to stay here. You have made each of my days as long as a hand is wide. My whole life is nothing in Your eyes. Everyone is only a breath, at best. They walk here and there like a shadow. They store up riches, not knowing who will gather them.

And now, Lord, what do I wait for? My hope is in You. Save me from all my sins. O Lord, hear my prayer and listen to my cry. Do not be quiet when You see my tears so I may have joy again before I go and am no more.

Reflection:

"Fall rouses the spirit of change to color your soul brave again."
– Angie Weiland Crosby

Goal Setting:

Be brave; ask God for the impossible visual. Note what you envision for your personal growth.

Spiritual: ____

____

____

____

____

____

____

____

Emotional: ____

____

____

____

____

____

____

____

Mental:

Physical:

Notes

Notes

Notes

A Fall Song of *Worship* and *Praise*

Inspired by Psalm 19, 28 & 32

Jehovah-'Ez-Lami — Lord my Strength and my Song.

Be glad in the Lord and be full of joy all you who are right with God. Sing for joy all you who are pure in heart for The Lord is our strength and safe cover.

Dear heavenly Father, the heavens tell of Your greatness and their vastness show the work of Your hand. Day to day, Your creation speaks of Your greatness as it rises from one end of the heavens to the other.

You are faithful to forgive the guilt of my sin. You are my hiding place. The place where I am safe and where I gain strength. Your songs of freedom surround me. Because I trust in You, I am embraced by Your loving-kindness.

Your Word is perfect, giving new strength to every soul. Your Word is right, giving joy to the heart. Your Word is pure, giving light to the eyes. The fear of You, O Lord is pure, lasting forever. You are always true and right in how You judge. Your Word is worth more than gold.

In obeying and choosing to live Your way, there is great reward. So please forgive my sins that I do not see. And keep me from sinning as I go my way. Do not let any sins rule over me. Let the words of my mouth and the desires of my heart be pleasing in Your eyes, O Lord, my Rock and the One Who saves me.

You are faithful to forgive the guilt of my sin. You are my hiding place. The place where I am safe and where I gain strength. Your songs of freedom surround me. Because I trust in You, I am embraced by Your loving-kindness.

Be glad in the Lord and be full of joy all you who are right with God. Sing for joy all you who are pure in heart for The Lord is our strength and safe cover.

Response:

A Fall Song of *Worship* and *Praise*

Highlight and Respond below

Inspired by Psalm 19, 28 & 32

Jehovah-'Ez-Lami – Lord my Strength and my Song.

Be glad in the Lord and be full of joy all you who are right with God. Sing for joy all you who are pure in heart for The Lord is our strength and safe cover.

Dear heavenly Father, the heavens tell of Your greatness and their vastness show the work of Your hand. Day to day, Your creation speaks of Your greatness as it rises from one end of the heavens to the other.

You are faithful to forgive the guilt of my sin. You are my hiding place. The place where I am safe and where I gain strength. Your songs of freedom surround me. Because I trust in You, I am embraced by Your loving-kindness.

Your Word is perfect, giving new strength to every soul. Your Word is right, giving joy to the heart. Your Word is pure, giving light to the eyes. The fear of You, O Lord is pure, lasting forever. You are always true and right in how You judge. Your Word is worth more than gold.

In obeying and choosing to live Your way, there is great reward. So please forgive my sins that I do not see. And keep me from sinning as I go my way. Do not let any sins rule over me. Let the words of my mouth and the desires of my heart be pleasing in Your eyes, O Lord, my Rock and the One Who saves me.

You are faithful to forgive the guilt of my sin. You are my hiding place. The place where I am safe and where I gain strength. Your songs of freedom surround me. Because I trust in You, I am embraced by Your loving-kindness.

Be glad in the Lord and be full of joy all you who are right with God. Sing for joy all you who are pure in heart for The Lord is our strength and safe cover.

Reflection:

> *"Thanks for the reminder that change can be beautiful."*
> – Jane Lee Logan

Memory and Cognition:

Within these leaves Note the times when you felt grateful for the beauty and brilliance of the season.

Within the leaves, name the beautiful ways God has shown up for you.

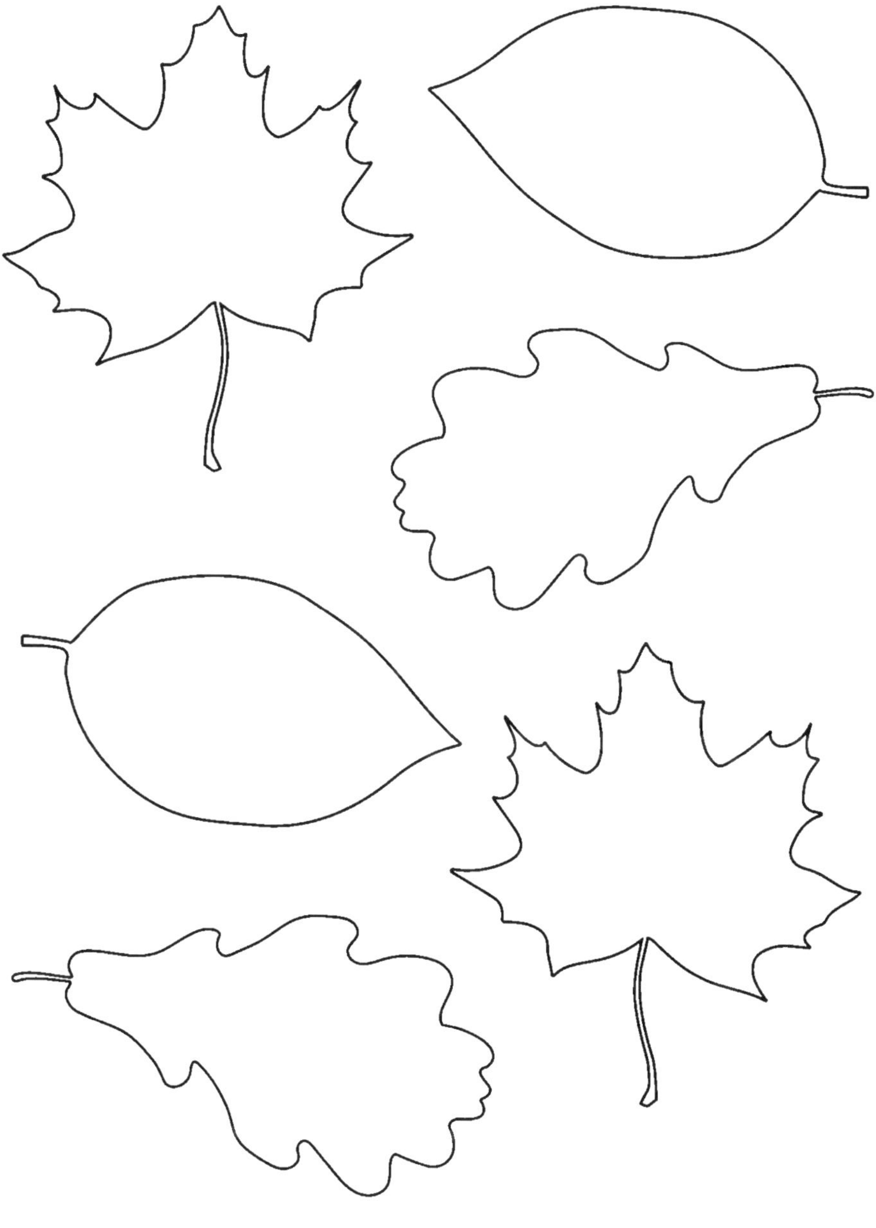

Notes

Notes

Notes

A Fall Prayer of *Petition* and *Blessing*

Inspired by Psalm 5, 14, 52, 53 & 130

Jehovah-Go'el – The Lord our Redeemer.

Hear my words, O Lord.

In the morning, O Lord, You will hear my voice. Think about my crying. Hear my cry for help, my King and my God. For I pray to you. In the morning I will lay my prayers before You and will look up for You are my Redeemer.

Hear my words, O Lord.

You are not a God Who is pleased with what is bad. The sinful cannot be with You. The proud cannot stand before You. You hate all who do wrong and those who lie.

Will those who sin never learn? They eat up people like they eat up bread. They do not call on Your name. They live in much fear.

Hear my words, O Lord.

My heart is heavy for those who choose to live foolishly as if there is no God. Their ways are sinful and they continue to do bad things. There is no one who does good.

God, You look down from heaven at us to see if there is anyone who understands and looks for You. And we have all turned back to sin.

Is there no one who does good, not even one? Do those who sin have understanding? This is why they do not call upon You? Why do we take pride in wrongdoing when we know Your loving kindness lasts all day long?

Our tongue makes plans to destroy like a sharp knife. We love what is bad more than what is good and we speak lies more than we speak the truth. We love words that destroy. There we are, in much fear, when there is nothing to be afraid of. Instead, we are put to shame because You have turned away from us.

Hear my words, O Lord.

In the morning, I will lay my prayers before You and will look up for You are my Redeemer.

Response:

A Fall Prayer of *Petition* and *Blessing*

Highlight and Respond below

Inspired by Psalm 5, 14, 52, 53 & 130

Jehovah-Go'el – The Lord our Redeemer.

Hear my words, O Lord.

In the morning, O Lord, You will hear my voice. Think about my crying. Hear my cry for help, my King and my God. For I pray to you. In the morning I will lay my prayers before You and will look up for You are my Redeemer.

Hear my words, O Lord.

You are not a God Who is pleased with what is bad. The sinful cannot be with You. The proud cannot stand before You. You hate all who do wrong and those who lie.

Will those who sin never learn? They eat up people like they eat up bread. They do not call on Your name. They live in much fear.

Hear my words, O Lord.

My heart is heavy for those who choose to live foolishly as if there is no God. Their ways are sinful and they continue to do bad things. There is no one who does good.

God, You look down from heaven at us to see if there is anyone who understands and looks for You. And we have all turned back to sin.

Is there no one who does good, not even one? Do those who sin have understanding? This is why they do not call upon You? Why do we take pride in wrongdoing when we know Your loving kindness lasts all day long?

Our tongue makes plans to destroy like a sharp knife. We love what is bad more than what is good and we speak lies more than we speak the truth. We love words that destroy. There we are, in much fear, when there is nothing to be afraid of. Instead, we are put to shame because You have turned away from us.

Hear my words, O Lord.

In the morning, I will lay my prayers before You and will look up for You are my Redeemer.

Reflection:

> *"We are what we repeatedly do. Excellence, then, is not an act, but a habit."* – Aristotle

Stress Management:

In a season of life that brings change, circle the word that best represents your feelings around that change.

- Welcoming
- Overwhelming
- Manageable
- Challenging

According to Aristotle, excellence is a habit developed by intentional practice and good choice.

No matter if you welcome change or you are overwhelmed by change, having healthy habits is necessary to navigate wisely through change.

Reflect on a healthy habit that has come about with a season of change.

What healthy habits do you think are necessary to navigate through a season of change?

How can my stress strengthen my faith

Notes

Notes

A Fall Song of *Worship* and *Praise*

Inspired by Psalm 33, 35 & 36

Jehovah-M'gaddishcem - Lord my Sanctifier

I am Jehovah who makes you holy. Exodus 31:13b (TLB)

Song of Praise to the Lord my Sanctifier

The heavens were made by the Word of the Lord. All the stars were made by the breath of His mouth. He gathers the waters of the sea together as in a bag. He places the waters in storehouses. Let all the earth fear the Lord. Let all the people of the world honor Him. For He spoke, and it was done. He spoke with strong words, and it stood strong. The Lord brings the plans of nations to nothing. He wrecks the plans of the people but the plans of the Lord stand forever. The plans of His heart stand through the future of all people.

Happy am I for He has chosen me for His own. My tongue will tell about how right and good God is, and about His praise all day long. My soul will be happy and full of joy because He did not give up on me.

But, My sin speaks loudly. Within my heart, I still hold fast to sin. I lose fear of my God. In my own eyes, I make much of myself. I hate the sin in my life. My words are false. I lie to myself. I have stopped being wise and doing good. My plans are for wrongdoing and my path is not good.

Why do I get such pleasure in my sin? Why do I not hate what is bad?

I put my head down in sorrow; You have seen it, O Lord. Do not keep quiet. O Lord, do not be far from me. Come and help me. Fight for me, my God and my Lord. Say what is right or wrong with me, O Lord my God, because You are right and good. Put in me a desire to tell about how right and good You are, and a longing to praise You all day long. All that I am, may it be a reflection of Your holiness.

O Lord, Your loving kindness goes to the heavens. You are as faithful as the sky is high. You are as right and good as mountains are big. When You judge, You are as fair as a sea is deep. My life came from You. In Your light I see light. Keep on giving Your loving kindness to me. Do not give up on me. Do not let the foot of pride come near me. Let Your presence be upon me as a reflection of Your holiness.

I will sing for joy and praise Your holy name with a new song. You are faithful and good to me. My tongue will tell about how right and good You are and about Your praise all day long. My soul will be happy and full of joy because You did not give up on me. Let Your presence stay with me

Response:

A Fall Song of *Worship* and *Praise*

Highlight and Respond below

Inspired by Psalm 33, 35 & 36

Jehovah-M'gaddishcem - Lord my Sanctifier

I am Jehovah who makes you holy. Exodus 31:13b (TLB)

Song of Praise to the Lord my Sanctifier

The heavens were made by the Word of the Lord. All the stars were made by the breath of His mouth. He gathers the waters of the sea together as in a bag. He places the waters in storehouses. Let all the earth fear the Lord. Let all the people of the world honor Him. For He spoke, and it was done. He spoke with strong words, and it stood strong. The Lord brings the plans of nations to nothing. He wrecks the plans of the people but the plans of the Lord stand forever. The plans of His heart stand through the future of all people.

Happy am I for He has chosen me for His own. My tongue will tell about how right and good God is, and about His praise all day long. My soul will be happy and full of joy because He did not give up on me.

But, My sin speaks loudly. Within my heart, I still hold fast to sin. I lose fear of my God. In my own eyes, I make much of myself. I hate the sin in my life. My words are false. I lie to myself. I have stopped being wise and doing good. My plans are for wrongdoing and my path is not good.

Why do I get such pleasure in my sin?
Why do I not hate what is bad?

I put my head down in sorrow; You have seen it, O Lord. Do not keep quiet. O Lord, do not be far from me. Come and help me. Fight for me, my God and my Lord. Say what is right or wrong with me, O Lord my God, because You are right and good. Put in me a desire to tell about how right and good You are, and a longing to praise You all day long. All that I am, may it be a reflection of Your holiness.

O Lord, Your loving kindness goes to the heavens. You are as faithful as the sky is high. You are as right and good as mountains are big. When You judge, You are as fair as a sea is deep. My life came from You. In Your light I see light. Keep on giving Your loving kindness to me. Do not give up on me. Do not let the foot of pride come near me. Let Your presence be upon me as a reflection of Your holiness.

I will sing for joy and praise Your holy name with a new song. You are faithful and good to me. My tongue will tell about how right and good You are and about Your praise all day long. My soul will be happy and full of joy because You did not give up on me. Let Your presence stay with me

Reflection:

> *"Let autumn leaves fall to the depth of my soul, a reminder to live with wisdom aglow."* – Angie Weiland Crosby

Personal Growth:

In Proverbs these Attributes of Wisdom are found.

Choose 5 Attributes to reference in Proverbs (The Message Bible)

In the leaves on the next page write the attribute, the biblical reference and how you desire to apply it to your personal growth in wisdom.

- Hopeful
- Humility
- Perspective
- Compassion
- God honoring
- Knowing what's important
- Love of knowledge
- Ability to judge well
- Fairness
- Patience
- Moral reasoning
- Social know-how
- Decision making based in reason not emotion
- Chastity

Notes

Notes

Notes

Notes

A Fall Prayer of *Petition* and *Blessing*

Inspired by Psalm 51, 65, 69 & 70

Prayer of the Sinner

O God, hurry to take me out of trouble. Hurry to help me!

Take away my wrongdoing because of the greatness of Your loving pity. Wash me inside and out from my wrongdoing and make me clean from my sin. For I know my wrongdoing and my sin is always in front of me. I have sinned against You and You only. I have done what is sinful in Your eyes. You are always right when You speak, and fair when You judge.

O God, take away my sin and cleanse me.

Wash me and I will be whiter than snow. Make me joyful and happy. Favor me because of Your loving kindness. Let me always look for You. Let me be glad in You. For I long to experience the full joy of Your forgiveness.

I was born in sin and lived in sin from my very beginning. Your desire is for truth to be rooted deep within my heart and for me to know wisdom in the hidden part. But I am poor and in need.

Hurry to me, O God! You are my Help and the One Who takes me out of trouble. O Lord, do not wait.

Save me, for the waters have almost taken my life. I have come into deep waters where floods come over me. I have gone down into the deep mud and there is no place to put my feet. I have cried until I am tired. My mouth is dry. My eyes are weak. You know how foolish I am. My sins are not hidden from You.

Answer me with Your saving truth in Your great loving-kindness, O God. Take me out of the mud and do not let me go down again. Guard me from those who hate me. Pluck me from the floodwaters and keep them from covering me. Do not let the sea swallow me up. Do not let the deep hole close its mouth over me. Answer me, O Lord, for Your loving-kindness is good. I am suffering and in pain. Save me and set me up on high. I will praise Your name with song and I will give You great honor with much thanks.

May heaven, earth, the seas and all the things that move in them give thanks to You.

You answer me in the way that is right and good. It's Your forgiveness and salvation I seek. You are the hope of all the ends of the earth and of the farthest seas. You have built the mountains by Your strength. You are dressed with power. You quiet the storm of the seas, the sound of its waves and the noise of the people. You make morning and evening call out for joy. It is Your great works that make all stand in awe.

O God, take away my sin and cleanse me. Wash me and I will be whiter than snow. Make me joyful and happy. Favor me because of Your loving-kindness. Let me always look for You. Let me be glad in You. For I long to experience the full joy of Your forgiveness.

Response:

A Fall Prayer of *Petition* and *Blessing*

Highlight and Respond below

Inspired by Psalm 51, 65, 69 & 70

Prayer of the Sinner

O God, hurry to take me out of trouble. Hurry to help me!

Take away my wrongdoing because of the greatness of Your loving pity. Wash me inside and out from my wrongdoing and make me clean from my sin. For I know my wrongdoing and my sin is always in front of me. I have sinned against You and You only. I have done what is sinful in Your eyes. You are always right when You speak, and fair when You judge.

O God, take away my sin and cleanse me.

Wash me and I will be whiter than snow. Make me joyful and happy. Favor me because of Your loving kindness. Let me always look for You. Let me be glad in You. For I long to experience the full joy of Your forgiveness.

I was born in sin and lived in sin from my very beginning. Your desire is for truth to be rooted deep within my heart and for me to know wisdom in the hidden part. But I am poor and in need.

Hurry to me, O God! You are my Help and the One Who takes me out of trouble. O Lord, do not wait.

Save me, for the waters have almost taken my life. I have come into deep waters where floods come over me. I have gone down into the deep mud and there is no place to put my feet. I have cried until I am tired. My mouth is dry. My eyes are weak. You know how foolish I am. My sins are not hidden from You.

Answer me with Your saving truth in Your great loving-kindness, O God. Take me out of the mud and do not let me go down again. Guard me from those who hate me. Pluck me from the floodwaters and keep them from covering me. Do not let the sea swallow me up. Do not let the deep hole close its mouth over me. Answer me, O Lord, for Your loving-kindness is good. I am suffering and in pain. Save me and set me up on high. I will praise Your name with song and I will give You great honor with much thanks.

May heaven, earth, the seas and all the things that move in them give thanks to You.

You answer me in the way that is right and good. It's Your forgiveness and salvation I seek. You are the hope of all the ends of the earth and of the farthest seas. You have built the mountains by Your strength. You are dressed with power. You quiet the storm of the seas, the sound of its waves and the noise of the people. You make morning and evening call out for joy. It is Your great works that make all stand in awe.

O God, take away my sin and cleanse me. Wash me and I will be whiter than snow. Make me joyful and happy. Favor me because of Your loving-kindness. Let me always look for You. Let me be glad in You. For I long to experience the full joy of Your forgiveness.

Reflection:

"Believe in your fall. It's paving a new way for your climb."
– Angie Weiland Crosby

Healing:

Make a list of your petitions; "I really want God to..."

What big dreams do you have for a fresh start?

Describe what your new way looks like

What are three things that I could have done differently

What are you doing today for eternity?

Write a forgiving message to yourself

Notes

Notes

Notes

A Fall Song of *Worship* and *Praise*

Inspired by Psalm 105, 106 & 108

Jehovah-Eli – Lord my God

I give thanks to You, Lord, my God! I, your servant and chosen one, will call upon Your holy name.

I will talk of all Your wondrous works and glorify Your holy name. My heart will rejoice for it is You I seek and Your strength I need. I will sing this psalm, O Lord, and seek Your face each morning! I will remember Your marvelous works and wonders.

With the rising of the sun, I will give You praise. I will continue to sing praises to You until my day is done. For I have experienced mercy that's shown greatly above the heavens. Your truth reaches to the clouds.

Lord my God, may Your name be exalted above the heavens and may Your glory shine above all the earth.

I give thanks to You, Lord, my God, for You are so good! Your mercy endures forever. Remember me, O Lord with Your favor. Visit me with Your salvation that I may rejoice in the gladness of Your glory and Your inheritance.

Your love, God, is my song and I will never stop singing it from Your holy mountains.

Response:

A Fall Song of *Worship* and *Praise*

Highlight and Respond below

Inspired by Psalm 105, 106 & 108

Jehovah-Eli – Lord my God

I give thanks to You, Lord, my God! I, your servant and chosen one, will call upon Your holy name.

I will talk of all Your wondrous works and glorify Your holy name. My heart will rejoice for it is You I seek and Your strength I need. I will sing this psalm, O Lord, and seek Your face each morning! I will remember Your marvelous works and wonders.

With the rising of the sun, I will give You praise. I will continue to sing praises to You until my day is done. For I have experienced mercy that's shown greatly above the heavens. Your truth reaches to the clouds.

Lord my God, may Your name be exalted above the heavens and may Your glory shine above all the earth.

I give thanks to You, Lord, my God, for You are so good! Your mercy endures forever. Remember me, O Lord with Your favor. Visit me with Your salvation that I may rejoice in the gladness of Your glory and Your inheritance.

Your love, God, is my song and I will never stop singing it from Your holy mountains.

Reflection:

> *"Gratitude is the healthiest of all human emotions. The more you express gratitude for what you have the more likely you will have even more to express gratitude for."* – ZIG ZIGLAR

Gratitude:

What are you grateful for?

It's natural to reflect on broader, life-level things, but also take a moment to reflect on smaller moments of gratitude – something brief and fleeting that you valued, but if not noted, may otherwise be forgotten. Write within the leaves.

Notes

Notes

Notes

A Fall Prayer of *Petition* and *Blessing*

Inspired by Psalm 132,134 &139

Jehovah-Nissi – Banner.

I will give honor and thanks to the Lord. I will lift up my hands to the holy place and give thanks to the Lord. May the Lord bring good to me for He is the One Who made heaven and earth. When I am awake, I am still with Him. He looks through me and knows my heart, tries me and knows my thoughts. He sees any sinful way in me and leads me in the way that lasts forever.

O Lord, You have looked through me and have known me. You know when I sit down and when I get up. You understand my thoughts from far away. You look over me as I walk my path and as I lay down. You know all my ways very well.

Even before I speak a word, O Lord, You know it all. You have closed me in from behind as well as in front. You have laid Your hand upon me. All You know is too great for me. It is too much for me to understand. For You made the parts inside me. You put me together inside my mother. I will give thanks to You, for the greatness of the way I was made brings fear. Your works are great and my soul knows it very well. Your eyes saw me before I was put together. And all the days of my life were written in Your book before any of them came to be.

Your thoughts are of great worth to me, O God. How many there are! If I could number them, there would be more than all the sands of the earth.

I will give honor and thanks to the Lord. I will lift up my hands to the holy place and give thanks to the Lord. May the Lord bring good to me for He is the One Who made heaven and earth. When I am awake, I am still with Him. He looks through me and knows my heart, tries me and knows my thoughts. He sees any sinful way in me and leads me in the way that lasts forever.

For the Lord has chosen me. This is my resting place forever; here I will dwell, for I have desired it. My God will abundantly bless and will satisfy. I will shout for joy for the Lord has chosen me.

Response:

A Fall Prayer of *Petition* and *Blessing*

Highlight and Respond below

Inspired by Psalm 132,134 &139

Jehovah-Nissi – Banner.

I will give honor and thanks to the Lord. I will lift up my hands to the holy place and give thanks to the Lord. May the Lord bring good to me for He is the One Who made heaven and earth. When I am awake, I am still with Him. He looks through me and knows my heart, tries me and knows my thoughts. He sees any sinful way in me and leads me in the way that lasts forever.

O Lord, You have looked through me and have known me. You know when I sit down and when I get up. You understand my thoughts from far away. You look over me as I walk my path and as I lay down. You know all my ways very well.

Even before I speak a word, O Lord, You know it all. You have closed me in from behind as well as in front. You have laid Your hand upon me. All You know is too great for me. It is too much for me to understand. For You made the parts inside me. You put me together inside my mother. I will give thanks to You, for the greatness of the way I was made brings fear. Your works are great and my soul knows it very well. Your eyes saw me before I was put together. And all the days of my life were written in Your book before any of them came to be.

Your thoughts are of great worth to me, O God. How many there are! If I could number them, there would be more than all the sands of the earth.

I will give honor and thanks to the Lord. I will lift up my hands to the holy place and give thanks to the Lord. May the Lord bring good to me for He is the One Who made heaven and earth. When I am awake, I am still with Him. He looks through me and knows my heart, tries me and knows my thoughts. He sees any sinful way in me and leads me in the way that lasts forever.

For the Lord has chosen me. This is my resting place forever; here I will dwell, for I have desired it. My God will abundantly bless and will satisfy. I will shout for joy for the Lord has chosen me.

Reflection:

> *"If you wake up feeling fragile, remember that God is not, and then trust Him to be everything you need today."* – C.S. Lewis

Self-awareness:

Did you wake up feeling fragile? In a season of change, circumstances can create a feeling of vulnerability. As we try to navigate through change successfully, it's crucial to identify *why* the change entered your life.

Review the reasons below and circle the one that signifies the trigger for this change:

> Sequence or chapter of life: Did this change come about due to a traditional new phase of life? Teen years, college years, starting a career, etc.
>
> Specific monumental event: Was there a significant event at the center of this change? A graduation, a birth, a death, etc.
>
> Specific purpose: Sometimes, a change occurs that has real purpose — His purpose may not be apparent to us yet; this change can be brought on by something small, less defined, or even represented by an ongoing feeling.
>
> (Refer to *Excellence with Simple Elegance*, p103-105.)

Write a sentence about the reason you circled and how the change has affected your life. If the change was driven by purpose, write a sentence about how the awareness of a purpose-driven change has influenced the way you think about the change itself.

Think about the disciplines in your daily routine and any other disciplines that could be valuable to your faith journey. Share how each of these disciplines can help steady your heart in the midst of change.

Disciplines: Bible reading, church attendance, praying, worship, fasting, solitude, fellowship, tithing and journaling.

Discipline

Discipline

Discipline

Discipline

Discipline

Notes

Notes

A Fall Song of *Worship* and *Praise*

Inspired by Psalm 18

Jehovah-Misqabbi – Lord my High Tower

Song of Thanks for Being Kept Safe

The Lord is my strength, my rock and my safe place. He is the One Who takes me out of trouble. My God is my rock, in Whom I am safe. He is my safe covering, my saving strength and my strong tower. I call to the Lord, Who has the right to be praised and I am saved from those who hate me. I call to the Lord in my trouble. I cry to God for help. He hears my voice from His holy house. My cry for help reaches His ears.

Lord, You give me a safe place, because You are pleased with me. You live in me! How great is my Rock! Praise be to the You, Lord, Who saves me!

Before Him I was without blame. And I have kept myself from sin. So the Lord has paid me back for being right with Him, and for my hands being clean in His eyes. To the faithful, He shows Himself faithful. To those without blame, He shows Himself blameless. With the pure, He shows Himself pure. He makes my lamp bright. The Lord my God lights my darkness. With my God I can jump over a wall.

Lord, You give me a safe place, because You are pleased with me. You live in me! How great is my Rock! Praise be to You, O Lord, Who saves me!

Your way is perfect. You are a covering for all who go to You. This blessed covering is a safe place. You also give me the covering that saves me. Your right hand holds me up. Your care makes me great. You make the road wide for my steps and my feet have not tripped.

Lord, You live in me! How great is my Rock! Praise be to You, Who saves me! Yes, You lift me above those who rise up against me. You save me from those who want to hurt me. So I will give thanks to You, the Lord among the nations. And I will sing praises to Your name as You show loving kindness.

Oh! Let the heavens be glad and let the earth be full of joy. Let the sea and all that is in it make a loud noise. Let the fields and all that is in them be full of joy. Then, all the trees of the land will sing for joy before You. I am so glad! You, O Lord, my safe covering, my saving strength and my strong tower, are coming.

Response:

A Fall Song of Worship and Praise

Highlight and Respond below

Inspired by Psalm 18

Jehovah-Misqabbi – Lord my High Tower

____

____

____

Song of Thanks for Being Kept Safe

The Lord is my strength, my rock and my safe place. He is the One Who takes me out of trouble. My God is my rock, in Whom I am safe. He is my safe covering, my saving strength and my strong tower. I call to the Lord, Who has the right to be praised and I am saved from those who hate me. I call to the Lord in my trouble. I cry to God for help. He hears my voice from His holy house. My cry for help reaches His ears.

____

____

____

____

Lord, You give me a safe place, because You are pleased with me. You live in me! How great is my Rock! Praise be to the You, Lord, Who saves me!

Before Him I was without blame. And I have kept myself from sin. So the Lord has paid me back for being right with Him, and for my hands being clean in His eyes. To the faithful, He shows Himself faithful. To those without blame, He shows Himself blameless. With the pure, He shows Himself pure. He makes my lamp bright. The Lord my God lights my darkness. With my God I can jump over a wall.

Lord, You give me a safe place, because You are pleased with me. You live in me! How great is my Rock! Praise be to You, O Lord, Who saves me!

Your way is perfect. You are a covering for all who go to You. This blessed covering is a safe place. You also give me the covering that saves me. Your right hand holds me up. Your care makes me great. You make the road wide for my steps and my feet have not tripped.

Lord, You live in me! How great is my Rock! Praise be to You, Who saves me! Yes, You lift me above those who rise up against me. You save me from those who want to hurt me. So I will give thanks to You, the Lord among the nations. And I will sing praises to Your name as You show loving kindness.

Oh! Let the heavens be glad and let the earth be full of joy. Let the sea and all that is in it make a loud noise. Let the fields and all that is in them be full of joy. Then, all the trees of the land will sing for joy before You. I am so glad! You, O Lord, my safe covering, my saving strength and my strong tower, are coming.

Reflection:

> *"Autumn came adorned in change, and flying leaves dancing in rain."* – Angie Weiland Crosby

Emotional Expression:

Reflect on occasions you've danced in celebration of all that is good in your life.

For each occasion, choose a leaf to write adjectives summarizing the joy within that moment. Repeat for each occasion in each respective leaf.

Notes

Notes

Notes

A TIME FOR EVERYTHING

There is a time for everything, and a season
for every activity under the heavens;
a time to be born and a time to die,
a time to plant and a time to uproot,
a time to kill and a time to heal,
a time to tear down and a time to build,
a time to weep and a time to laugh,
a time to mourn and a time to dance,
a time to scatter stones and a time to gather them,
a time to embrace and a time to refrain from embracing,
a time to search and a time to give up,
a time to keep and a time to throw away,
a time to tear and a time to mend,
a time to be silent and a time to speak,
a time to love and a time to hate,
a time for war and a time for peace.

— ECCLESIASTES 3:1–8

TO CONTACT THE AUTHOR

Bonnie Liabenow is a passionate, committed, faith – driven woman. She is dedicated to providing encouragement in words of faith to women of all ages during all seasons of their lives. She has counseled women across the country in personal goal-setting, goal acquisition, and time management. Bonnie has also demonstrated a commitment to service, hard work and excellence through her professional career. In addition to serving her community as an author and teacher, she is also the Vice President of Core Communications International , and has been recognized as a successful 'Lady Farmer' by various reputable publications for her strides and best practices in the Christmas Tree farming industry. Prior to launching her professional career, she finished two years of biblical studies at Bethel College, and earned a bachelor of science degree in recreational therapy at Michigan State University. Bonnie is a proud wife, mother of three sons / two daughter-in-laws and finds complete joy in being 'Nana' to her six grandchildren.

Bonnie Liabenow is an inspirational speaker/life coach who delivers a powerful emotional message to women of faith. Invite Bonnie to lead your group to live intentionally, and to experience a new day with purpose and fulfillment.

Contact Bonnie at bliabenow@live.com
or at facebook.com/bonnieliabenow

Also by Bonnie Liabenow

Excellence with Simple Elegance

And it's companion workbook
The Study

JOURNALING THROUGH THE SEASONS

The new series of guided journals

Journaling through the Seasons: Fall & Faith

Journaling through the Seasons: Winter & Word

Journaling through the Seasons: Spring & Spirit

Journaling through the Seasons: Summer & Sonship